All Kinds of Friends

My Friend Uses Leg Braces

by Kaitlyn Duling

Bullfrog Books

Ideas for Parents and Teachers

Bullfrog Books let children practice reading informational text at the earliest reading levels. Repetition, familiar words, and photo labels support early readers.

Before Reading

• Discuss the cover photo. What does it tell them?

• Look at the picture glossary together. Read and discuss the words.

Read the Book

• "Walk" through the book and look at the photos. Let the child ask questions. Point out the photo labels.

• Read the book to the child, or have him or her read independently.

After Reading

• Prompt the child to think more. Ask: Do you know someone who uses leg braces? What activities do you do together?

Bullfrog Books are published by Jump!
5357 Penn Avenue South
Minneapolis, MN 55419
www.jumplibrary.com

Library of Congress Cataloging-in-Publication Data

Names: Duling, Kaitlyn, author.
Title: My friend uses leg braces / by Kaitlyn Duling.
Description: Minneapolis, MN: Jump!, Inc., [2020]
Series: All kinds of friends
Audience: Age 5–8. | Audience: K to grade 3.
Includes bibliographical references and index.
Identifiers: LCCN 2018053635 (print)
LCCN 2018057807 (ebook)
ISBN 9781641287432 (ebook)
ISBN 9781641287418 (hardcover : alk. paper)
ISBN 9781641287425 (pbk.)
Subjects: LCSH: Children with disabilities—Juvenile literature. | Orthopedic braces—Juvenile literature. Leg—Abnormalities—Juvenile literature.
Classification: LCC HV903 (ebook)
LCC HV903 .D85 2019 (print) | DDC 305.9/083083—dc23
LC record available at https://lccn.loc.gov/2018053635

Editor: Susanne Bushman
Designer: Molly Ballanger

Photo Credits: Tad Saddoris, cover, 5, 23bl; duaneellison/iStock, 1, 4, 22tl, 22tr, 23tl, 24; Dan Race/Shutterstock, 3; Science Photo Library/Getty, 6–7; Olesia Bilkei/Shutterstock, 8–9, 14–15; Jaren Jai Wicklund/Shutterstock, 10, 11, 22bl; Sally Anderson Weather/Alamy, 12–13; Ahturner/Shutterstock, 16, 17, 23br; Huntstock/Getty, 18–19; Special Olympics, 20–21; jarenwicklund/iStock, 22br; Tony Stock/Shutterstock, 23tr.

Printed in the United States of America at Corporate Graphics in North Mankato, Minnesota.

Table of Contents

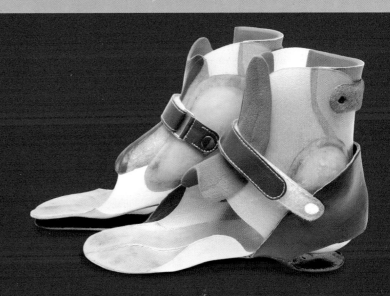

On the Move

These are leg braces.

What do they do?

leg brace

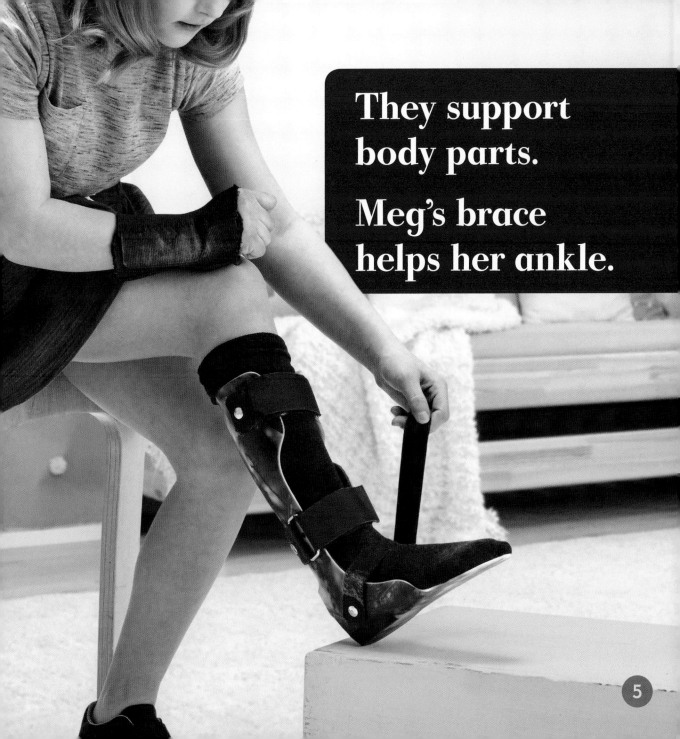

They support body parts.
Meg's brace helps her ankle.

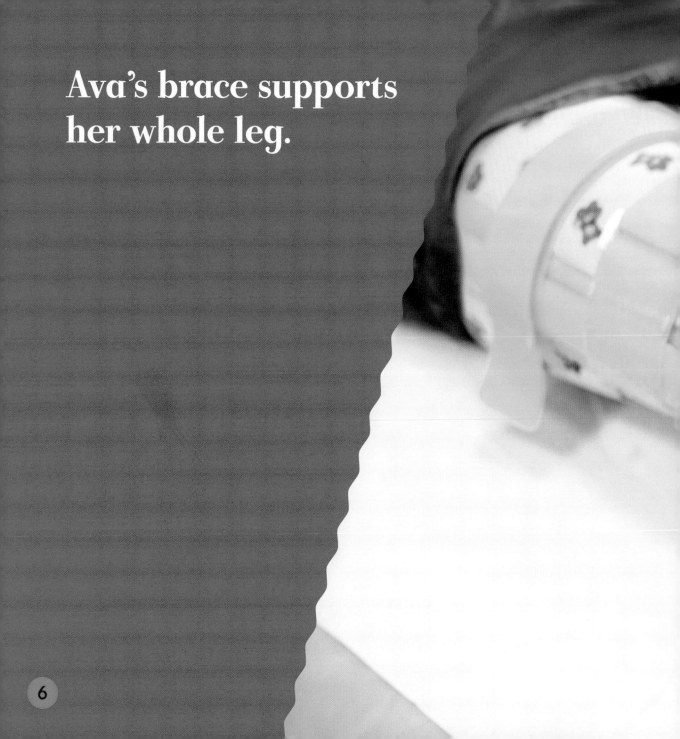

Ava's brace supports her whole leg.

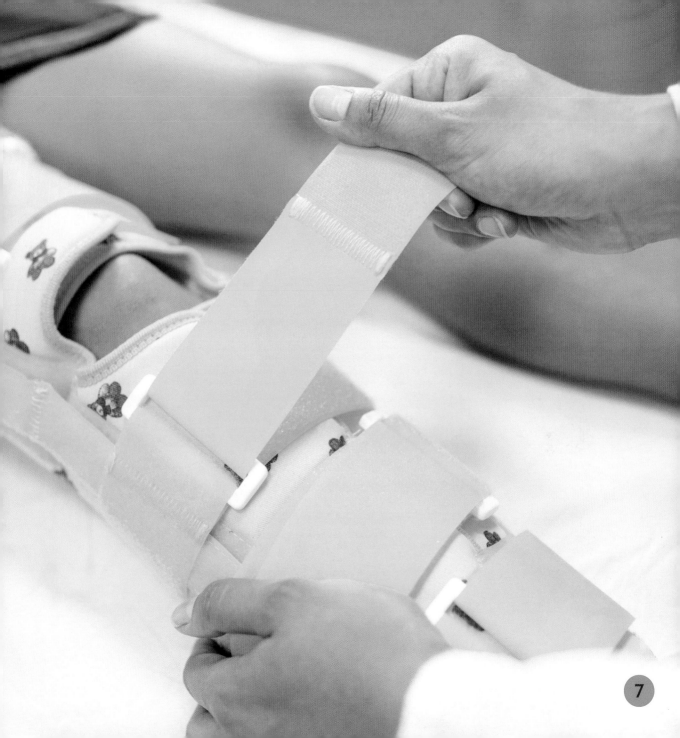

Val is in my class.

She wears leg braces.

We play!

Fun!

Mike's dad helps!
They get ready.

wheelchair

Mike goes to school.
He uses a wheelchair.

leg
brace

Wes wears one leg brace.
He goes to the beach.
He looks for seashells.
Nice!

Jake does exercises.
They help his muscles.
He gets stronger.

Del's sister wears
leg braces.

She uses a walker, too.

It helps her move.

walker

17

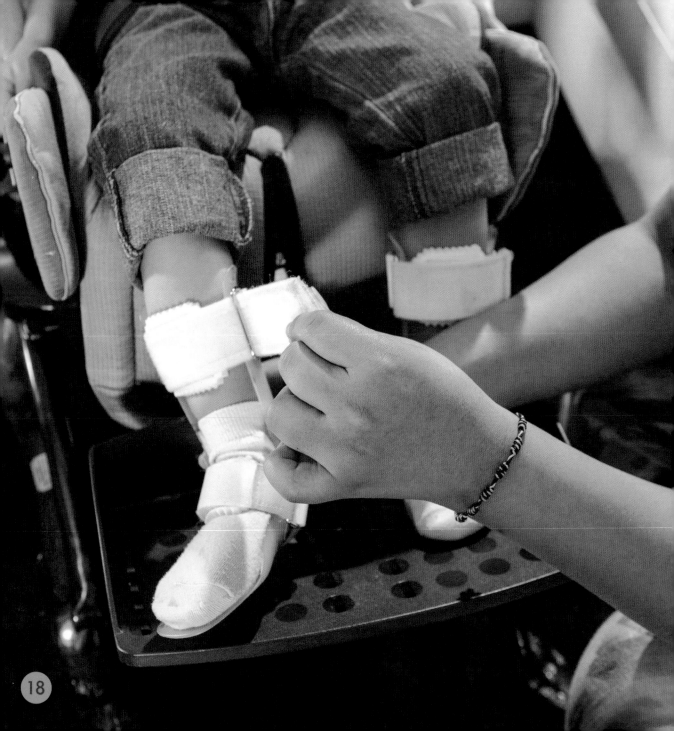

Leg braces come
in many sizes.

Tess grows.

She gets bigger braces!

Cool!

We run.

We play.

Ready? Let's go!

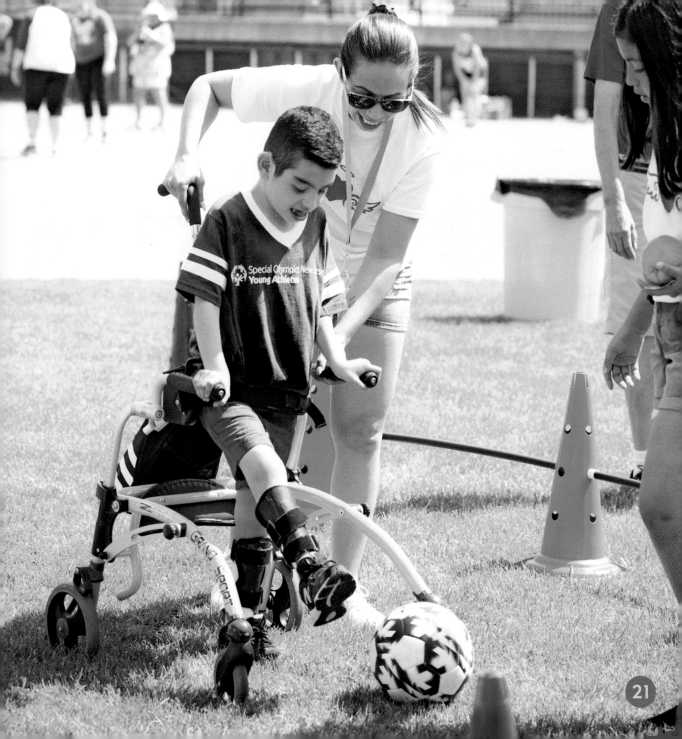

Helpful Tools

canes
Canes help people stay stable and balanced while they walk or run.

leg braces
Leg braces help support weak legs or ankles.

walker
A walker supports one's weight while he or she walks or runs. Some have wheels.

wheelchair
People who cannot walk sit in a wheelchair. They can push the wheels to move. Other wheelchairs have motors.

Picture Glossary

leg braces
Tools that attach to legs to help a person walk, stand, balance, and grow.

muscles
Tissues that are connected to a skeleton and pull on bones to make them move.

support
To help by bearing the weight of something.

walker
A device that helps support someone while he or she walks.

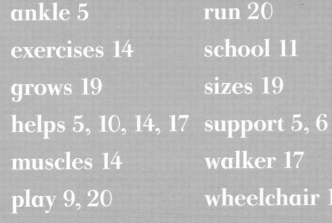

To Learn More

Finding more information is as easy as 1, 2, 3.

❶ Go to www.factsurfer.com

❷ Enter "myfrienduseslegbraces" into the search box.

❸ Choose your book to see a list of websites.